HANADEKA CLUB®
BY YONEO MORITA

Animal Friends

This book is full of the cutest animals around! Cuddle up to puppies, kittens, rabbits, and more. Turn the page and get to know them!

Maine Coon

FAST FACT

Weight: 9 to 18 pounds
(4 to 8 kilograms)

Maine Coons come in many colors and patterns.

Hi! I am a Maine Coon. I like to live in the cold. My fur is thick. My tail is long and bushy. I have fur in my ears to keep them warm.

We Maine Coons like to hang out with you. We get along well with other cats, too. We even like dogs!

The Maine Coon is the state cat of Maine.

Ferret

FAST
FACTS

- Length: 18 to 24 inches
  (46 to 61 centimeters)
- Weight: 1 to 6 pounds
  (1 to 3 kilograms)

Ferrets are **nocturnal** (say it like this: nahk-tur-nul). This means they are more active at night.

I am a kind of weasel. Some people keep ferrets like me as pets.

I can learn to use a litter box like a cat. I can also learn to go for walks on a leash like a dog!

Shih Tzu

- Height: 8 to 11 inches (20 to 28 centimeters)
- Weight: 9 to 16 pounds (4 to 7 kilograms)

The name Shih Tzu means "lion."

Hi! I am a Shih Tzu. Say my name like this: sheed-zoo.

I am friendly and sweet. I like to be with people. I have a lot of energy and love to play. Do you have a ball I can chase?

Shih Tzus came from China.

Rabbit

- Length: 7 to 19 inches
  (18 to 48 centimeters)
- Weight: 2 to 3 pounds
  (1 kilogram)

A rabbit lives in a **burrow**. These are holes or tunnels in the ground.

I am a bunny, which is a baby rabbit. My fur is long and soft. It can be brown, white, gray, black, or striped. My long ears help me listen for animals that like to chase me.

I am very curious. What is that over there?

A rabbit's teeth never stop growing.

Jack Russell Terrier

- Height: 10 to 15 inches (25 to 38 centimeters)
- Weight: 14 to 18 pounds (6 to 8 kilograms)

Jack Russell terriers are hunting dogs.

Jack Russell terriers like me love to have fun! I can be trained to do neat tricks. Barking and digging are two things I do very well.

I need a lot of exercise, too. Did you know that I can jump and climb?

Jack Russell terriers can live for 15 years or more.

French Bulldog

- Height: 11 to 13 inches
  (28 to 33 centimeters)
- Weight: 18 to 28 pounds
  (8 to 13 kilograms)

French bulldogs are also called "Frenchies."

Hi! I am a French bulldog. I am playful and lovable. I also want a lot of attention from you. Frenchies like me love to clown around, too.

I really like my human friends. Please do not leave me alone for too long!

Frenchies are easy to train. They are smart and learn quickly.

Hamster

- Length: 2 to 13 inches
  (5 to 34 centimeters)
- Weight: 3 to 4 ounces
  (85 to 113 grams)

Hamsters eat foods, like fruit, nuts, and berries.

Nice to meet you! I am a hamster. I have large cheek pouches where I put food. Then, I bring it home to eat later.

I am a **rodent**. This means my teeth grow all the time. I have to chew on hard things so my teeth do not get too long!

Most hamsters have white, black, brown, gray, yellow, or red fur.

Abyssinian

- Length: medium to long
- Weight: 8 to 17 pounds (4 to 8 kilograms)

Abyssinians are one of the oldest breeds of pet cats.

Hi! I am an Abyssinian. Say my name like this: ab-uh-sin-ee-in.

I am a loyal, smart cat. I like to spend a lot of time with my human friends. I get along well with other cats, too. I love to play!

These cats are also called "Abys."

Pig

- Length: 35 to 71 inches (89 to 180 centimeters), depending on the species
- Weight: 110 to 770 pounds (50 to 350 kilograms), depending on the species

Oink, oink! I am a piglet, which is a baby pig. Pigs are found almost everywhere in the world. Many people like to keep pigs like me on farms and as pets.

Rolling in the mud helps me to cool off. I am one of the smartest animals around. I can even learn to do tricks!

Poodle

FAST FACTS

- Height: 10 to 27 inches (25 to 69 centimeters)
- Weight: 6 to 70 pounds (3 to 32 kilograms)

Poodles are very smart.

Hi there! I am a Poodle. I love the water, and I am a great swimmer. Dogs like me have hair, not fur.

There are three kinds of Poodles: Standard, Miniature, and Toy. We are all different sizes. But we all love to have fun!

These dogs need a lot of love from their human friends.

Chipmunk

FAST FACTS

- Length: 7 to 12 inches (18 to 30 centimeters) including tail
- Weight: 1 to 5 ounces (28 to 142 grams)

Chipmunks have cheek pouches. They are used to carry food.

I am a chipmunk. Do I look a little bit like a mouse? I am a **rodent**, just like a mouse.

I live in a "house" under the ground called a burrow. My burrow has "rooms" and many long paths. I store food there for the cold winter months. Brrr!

A chipmunk **burrow** can be more than 11 feet (4 meters) long!

Welsh Corgi

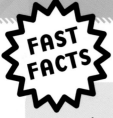
- Height: 10 to 12 inches (25 to 30 centimeters)
- Weight: 25 to 30 pounds (11 to 14 kilograms)

Welsh Corgis were used to **herd** sheep, horses, and cattle.

I am a Welsh Corgi. Say my name like this: welsh kor-gee.

I have short legs, but I am still a good jumper. I like to run and play. I am very smart and loyal, and I listen well. I protect my human friends, too!

Persian

- Length: Medium to long
- Weight: 10 to 11 pounds (4 to 5 kilograms)

You can barely hear Persians like me when we say hello! I have a soft meow. I am a quiet, sweet, and gentle cat. I have long fur that needs to be combed every day.

I love to play, but I do not like to jump too high or climb. I get along well with other cats and dogs, too!

Many people think that Persians came from ancient Egypt.

Chicken

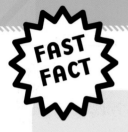

Height: 12 to 18 inches
(30 to 46 centimeters)

There are more chickens on Earth than people!

Cheep, cheep! I am a chick, which is a baby chicken. I am covered in soft, fluffy, yellow feathers. My feathers will change color as I get older.

We chicks like to peck at everything. What is that over there?

Chickens make different noises to talk to each other.

Mixed Breed Cat

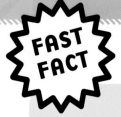
Length: Medium

A cat sleeps for about 16 hours every day.

Meow! I am a **mixed breed** cat. This means my parents are two different breeds. Mixed breeds like me come in many different sizes and colors.

I am curious, friendly, and lovable. I like to play, too. Do you have a string I can chase?

Cats can smell and hear much better than humans can.

Glossary

Burrow: a hole or tunnel dug in the ground by an animal

Herd: to gather together in a group

Mixed breed: an animal with parents of two different breeds

Nocturnal (nahk-tur-nul): active at night

Rodent: a small mammal with large front teeth that constantly grow and are used for chewing